HAWAII

BY ALICIA Z. KLEPEIS

BELLWETHER MEDIA • MINNEAPOLIS, MN

Blastoff! Discovery launches a new mission: reading to learn. Filled with facts and features, each book offers you an exciting new world to explore!

BLASTOFF! UNIVERSE

BLASTOFF! Beginners — GRADE K

BLASTOFF! READERS — GRADES 1-3

BLASTOFF! DISCOVERY — GRADE 4

This edition first published in 2022 by Bellwether Media, Inc.

No part of this publication may be reproduced in whole or in part without written permission of the publisher.
For information regarding permission, write to Bellwether Media, Inc.,
Attention: Permissions Department,
6012 Blue Circle Drive, Minnetonka, MN 55343.

Library of Congress Cataloging-in-Publication Data

Names: Klepeis, Alicia, 1971- author.
Title: Hawaii / by Alicia Z. Klepeis.
Description: Minneapolis, MN : Bellwether Media, Inc., 2022. |
    Series: Blastoff! Discovery: State profiles | Includes bibliographical
    references and index. | Audience: Ages 7-13 | Audience: Grades
    4-6 | Summary: "Engaging images accompany information about
    Hawaii. The combination of high-interest subject matter and
    narrative text is intended for students in grades 3 through 8"–
    Provided by publisher.
Identifiers: LCCN 2021019687 (print) | LCCN 2021019688 (ebook)
    | ISBN 9781644873823 (library binding) |
    ISBN 9781648341595 (ebook)
Subjects: LCSH: Hawaii–Juvenile literature.
Classification: LCC DU623.25 .K55 2022 (print) |
    LCC DU623.25 (ebook) | DDC 996.9–dc23
LC record available at https://lccn.loc.gov/2021019687
LC ebook record available at https://lccn.loc.gov/2021019688

Editor: Kate Moening   Designer: Andrea Schneider

Printed in the United States of America, North Mankato, MN.

TABLE OF CONTENTS

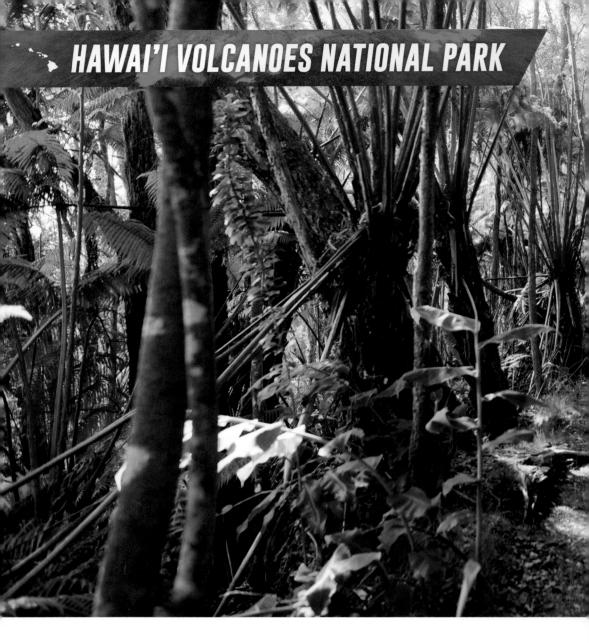

It is a warm winter morning when a school group arrives at Hawai'i **Volcanoes** National Park. After a quick stop at the visitor center, they head to the Kīlauea Iki Trail. They hike through a lush **rain forest**. The bright red wings of an apanane flash as the bird flits among the flowers. A happy-face spider rests on a leaf.

DIAMOND HEAD (LĒʻAHI)

IOLANI PALACE

NĀPALI COAST

PUNALUʻU BEACH

KĪLAUEA IKI TRAIL
HAWAIʻI VOLCANOES
NATIONAL PARK

The group has a picnic lunch on the trail. In the distance, steam rises out of openings in the earth. Later, the students get a chance to walk through a **lava tube**. Welcome to Hawaii!

NIIHAU

KAUAI

HAWAII

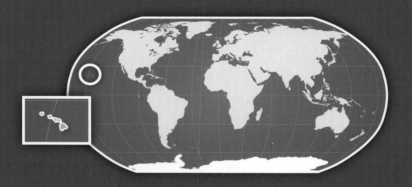

Hawaii is an **archipelago** located in the Pacific Ocean. This state is about 2,400 miles (3,862 kilometers) southwest of California. Hawaii covers 10,932 square miles (28,314 square kilometers), including ocean waters.

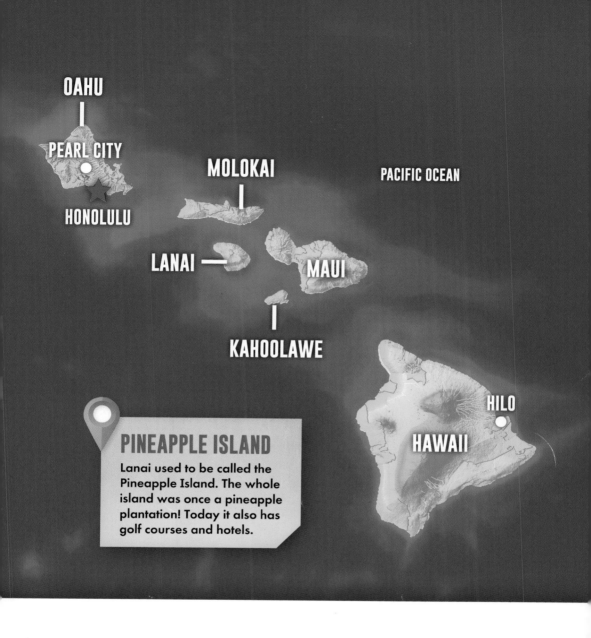

OAHU

PEARL CITY

HONOLULU

MOLOKAI

LANAI

MAUI

KAHOOLAWE

PACIFIC OCEAN

HILO

HAWAII

PINEAPPLE ISLAND

Lanai used to be called the Pineapple Island. The whole island was once a pineapple plantation! Today it also has golf courses and hotels.

Hawaii is the only state made of islands. It has 132 of them. The eight main ones are Hawaii, Maui, Oahu, Kauai, Molokai, Lanai, Niihau, and Kahoolawe. Hawaii is the biggest island in the state and in the country. It is also home to the world's biggest volcano, Mauna Loa. Honolulu, the capital and Hawaii's biggest city, is on Oahu.

HAWAII'S BEGINNINGS

DIAMOND HEAD
(LĒ'AHI), 1870S
OAHU

Hawaii's first residents came as early as 300 CE. They traveled from **Polynesia** in huge canoes. These early people fished and farmed. They lived in small communities. In 1778, British sea captain James Cook became the first European to arrive in Hawaii.

By 1810, a local king named Kamehameha had united the islands. White **missionaries** and traders soon came to the islands. Workers came from China, Japan, Korea, and other countries. They worked on sugar **plantations**. In the 1890s, American **colonists** overthrew Hawaii's last queen, Lili'uokalani. Hawaii became part of the U.S. in 1900 and the 50th state in 1959.

■ = NATIVE HAWAIIAN TRIBAL AREAS

NATIVE PEOPLE OF HAWAII

Unlike Native Americans, Native Hawaiians have a single language and culture. Some Native Hawaiians live in one of the state's 75 tribal areas.

NATIVE HAWAIIANS

- Original lands across all major islands but separated into four main chiefdoms (Hawai'i, Maui, O'ahu, Kaua'i) before King Kamehameha I united the archipelago
- More than 380,000 people in the state have some Native Hawaiian or Pacific Islander heritage
- Also called Kanaka Maoli and Kanaka 'Oiwi

Hawaii has many different landforms. The islands formed from numerous volcanoes. Only Kīlauea, Mauna Loa, and Lōʻihi are active today. Most islands are mountainous in the center and flatten near the coast. Several islands have rain forests and waterfalls. Kauai is home to Waimea **Canyon**, or the "Grand Canyon of the Pacific."

KĪLAUEA
MAUNA LOA
WAIMEA CANYON

WAIMEA CANYON

SPRING
HIGH: 81°F (27°C)
LOW: 67°F (19°C)

SUMMER
HIGH: 85°F (29°C)
LOW: 72°F (22°C)

FALL
HIGH: 85°F (29°C)
LOW: 71°F (22°C)

WINTER
HIGH: 80°F (27°C)
LOW: 66°F (19°C)

°F = degrees Fahrenheit
°C = degrees Celsius

BEACHES OF MANY COLORS

Several of Hawaii's beaches have black sand. The sand is made of crushed up lava. Hawaii also has beaches with green, red, and orange sand.

Hawaii has a **tropical** climate. Dry and rainy are the two main seasons. The rainy season is usually November to April. Temperatures do not vary much during the year. Hawaii faces danger from earthquakes, flooding, and **hurricanes**. The coastlines are also at risk of powerful waves called tsunamis.

11

Hawaii is home to a rich variety of wildlife. Hawaiian monk seals dive for eels and spiny lobsters off the coasts. Hawksbill turtles feed on crabs in the **coral reefs**. Seabirds such as black-footed albatrosses soar overhead.

Often found in Hawaii's cities, geckos feast on insects and plants. The Hawaiian hoary bat is the state's only native land mammal. It hunts for mosquitoes, moths, and other insects at night. Fiery red 'i'iwis, or scarlet honeycreepers, feed on the nectar of ohi'a flowers. Hawai'i 'amakihi call to each other in the treetops.

GOLD DUST DAY GECKO

'I'IWI

BANDED SPINY LOBSTER

HAWKSBILL TURTLE

HAWAII'S FUTURE: CORAL REEFS

Hawaii's coral reefs are declining, due to both climate change and overfishing. Many ocean animals cannot survive in unhealthy reefs. Hawaiian fishers will not be able to find the variety of fish they depend on. Tourism may also decline.

HAWAI'I 'AMAKIHI

Life Span: up to 12 years
Status: least concern

Hawai'i 'amakihi range =

LEAST CONCERN	NEAR THREATENED	VULNERABLE	ENDANGERED	CRITICALLY ENDANGERED	EXTINCT IN THE WILD	EXTINCT

Hawaii is more crowded than most other states. Over 1.4 million people live in the state. Most Hawaiians live in or near cities. Roughly 7 out of 10 Hawaiians live on Oahu.

KAILUA
OAHU

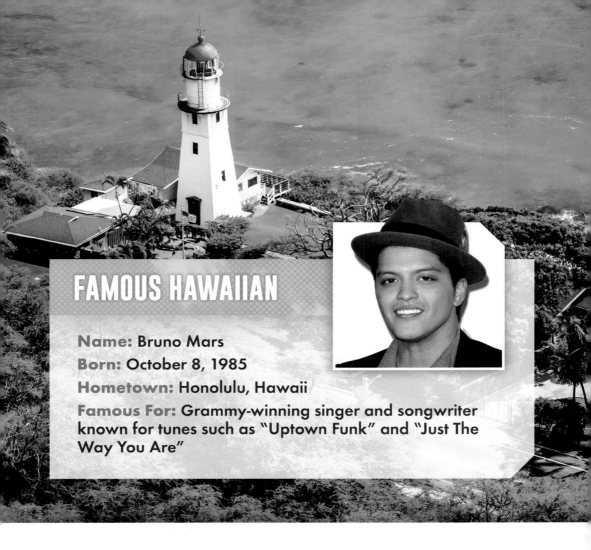

FAMOUS HAWAIIAN

Name: Bruno Mars

Born: October 8, 1985

Hometown: Honolulu, Hawaii

Famous For: Grammy-winning singer and songwriter known for tunes such as "Uptown Funk" and "Just The Way You Are"

There is no majority when it comes to Hawaiians' backgrounds. About one out of three people has Asian **heritage**. About one in four people is either Native Hawaiian alone or a mix of Native Hawaiian and other races. There are also large groups of people with European heritage and people of mixed race. About one in five Hawaiians is from another country. Many have come from the Philippines, China, Korea, and Japan.

15

Honolulu was a small fishing village for centuries. After Europeans arrived, it grew quickly. Traders and whalers came from around the world. Former plantation workers started businesses in the city. Honolulu became the capital of the Hawaiian kingdom in 1850. Today, Honolulu is Hawaii's largest city. **Tourism** and the military are important to its economy. It remains an important trade stop between Asia and North America.

Shops, restaurants, and art galleries in Honolulu's Chinatown celebrate Chinese **culture**. Iolani Palace gives a look into Hawaiian royalty's past. The Pearl Harbor National Memorial remembers lives lost in World War II.

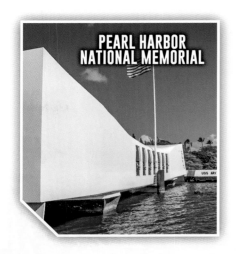

PEARL HARBOR NATIONAL MEMORIAL

WONDERFUL WAIKIKI

About 6 million people visit Honolulu's Waikiki Beach each year. People surf, snorkel, swim, and shop along Waikiki's 2-mile (3.2-kilometer) stretch.

WAIKIKI BEACH

17

PINEAPPLE FARM

Farming and fishing have been important to Hawaii since its earliest days. The state has rich soil for crops. Huge farms grow sugarcane, pineapples, coffee, and macadamia nuts. Cattle ranches are found on most islands. Tuna is the biggest catch for commercial fishers.

HAWAII'S FUTURE: AFFORDABLE HOUSING

Hawaii has the highest house prices of any state in the country. Lack of affordable housing will lead to rising homelessness. It will also hurt Hawaii's economy as people must spend more of their income on housing.

Tourism is the largest industry in Hawaii.
Some people work in parks, hotels, or golf courses.
Hawaiian factory workers make printed fabric and
clothing. Some also produce Hawaiian food items
including tropical fruit juices or candies.

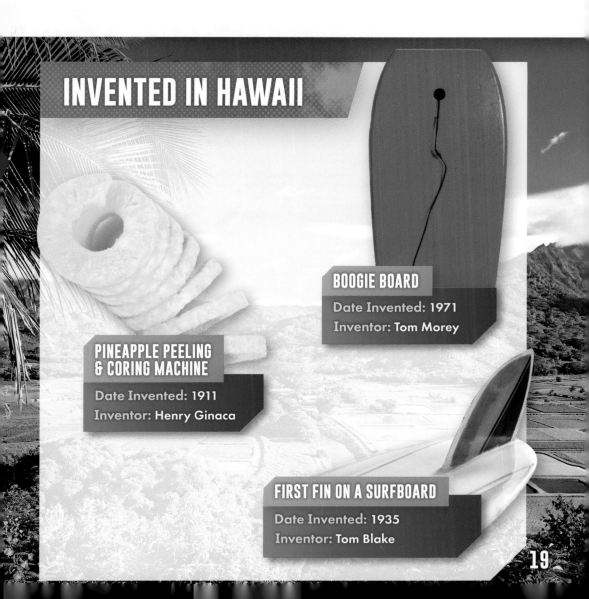

INVENTED IN HAWAII

BOOGIE BOARD
Date Invented: 1971
Inventor: Tom Morey

PINEAPPLE PEELING & CORING MACHINE
Date Invented: 1911
Inventor: Henry Ginaca

FIRST FIN ON A SURFBOARD
Date Invented: 1935
Inventor: Tom Blake

MAHI-MAHI

Seafood is an important part of many Hawaiian dishes. *Lomi-lomi* salmon includes salmon, sweet onions, and tomatoes. Mahi-mahi and tuna are also popular fish. Favorite fresh fruits include coconuts, mangoes, and pineapples. Hawaiians also eat locally grown purple sweet potatoes and Okinawan spinach.

A COOL TREAT

Shave ice is a well-loved dessert in Hawaii. Finely shaved ice is topped with colorful sweet syrup. Popular flavors include strawberry, mango, and passion fruit. Some people even put adzuki beans on top!

Hawaii's food reflects its Polynesian heritage. A luau is a **traditional** Hawaiian feast. Cooks roast a whole pig slowly in an underground oven. *Poi* is a side dish made from a starchy root called **taro**. It is slightly sweet. A popular luau dessert is *haupia*, a coconut pudding. Hawaiians enjoy drinking local coffee and tropical fruit juices.

POI

HAUPIA

FRUIT & MANGO DIP

4 SERVINGS

More than 500 kinds of mango grow on the Hawaiian Islands. Try this dip as a snack or a light meal! Have an adult help you.

INGREDIENTS

1 ripe mango

2/3 cup plain yogurt (not fat-free)

3/4 cup pineapple chunks

10 strawberries

2 kiwifruit

1 banana

wooden or bamboo skewers (optional)

DIRECTIONS

1. Peel the mango and remove the pit. Put the flesh into a bowl and mash it until mostly smooth.

2. Add the yogurt to the mashed mango. Stir until well combined.

3. Remove the stems from the strawberries. Peel the kiwifruit and cut it into chunks. Peel the banana and cut it into 1-inch-long pieces.

4. Place pieces of the different types of fruit onto the skewers or forks.

5. Dunk the fruit into the mango dip. Enjoy!

SPORTS AND ENTERTAINMENT

SNORKELING

Hawaii's warm climate and beautiful landscape provide many fun activities. Some people surf and swim along the coastline. Others scuba dive and **snorkel** in the warm waters. People race large canoes throughout the archipelago. Many people hike and camp in Hawaii's state and national parks.

Hawaiians take pride in their music and dance. Students of all ages can study hula. This traditional dance appears in ceremonies and storytelling in Hawaiian culture. Honolulu has many outdoor venues to enjoy live music. The city's Aloha Stadium hosts events from monster truck rallies to football games to concerts.

SNOW IN HAWAII

The island of Hawaii has tall mountains including Mauna Kea. Mountain peaks can be snow covered. There are no ski lifts. But people sometimes drive to the summit for a snowboarding run!

NOTABLE SPORTS TEAM

Hawaii Rainbow Wahine

Sport: Big West Conference (women's volleyball)

Started: 1972

Place of Play: Stan Sheriff Center

LEI DAY

Chinese New Year is one of the year's first big celebrations in Hawaii. Red lanterns light the streets of Honolulu's Chinatown. There are parades and fireworks displays. May 1 is **Lei** Day across the islands. People enjoy local food, watch hula performances, and learn how to make leis.

The Kaua'i Chocolate & Coffee Festival takes place each October. People taste samples and learn about these locally produced items. Near the year's end, surfers from around the world compete in the Vans Triple Crown. It takes place on Oahu's North Shore. Hawaiians celebrate their stunning state throughout the year!

VANS TRIPLE CROWN

KING KAMEHAMEHA DAY

On June 11, Hawaiians celebrate how King Kamehameha I united the islands into one kingdom. This festival is held across the Hawaiian Islands. Block parties and floral parades are part of the festivities.

1941

Pearl Harbor is
attacked by Japan

300 TO 700 CE

Polynesians from the
Marquesas Islands arrive
in the Hawaiian Islands

1891

Lili'uokalani
becomes queen of
the islands

1778

British explorer James
Cook lands in the
Hawaiian Islands

1900

Hawaii becomes
a territory of the
United States

1992

Hurricane Iniki hits the island of Kauai and causes much damage

2013

Mazie K. Hirono becomes Hawaii's first female senator

2006

An earthquake shakes the Hawaiian Islands

1959

Hawaii becomes the 50th U.S. state

2018

Kīlauea volcano erupts, destroying 700 homes

Nickname: The Aloha State

Motto: *Ua Mau ke Ea o ka ʻĀina i ka Pono;*
"The Life of the Land Is Perpetuated in Righteousness"

Date of Statehood: August 21, 1959 (the 50th state)

Capital City: Honolulu ⭐

Other Major Cities: Pearl City, Hilo, Waipahu

Area: 10,932 square miles (28,314 square kilometers);
Hawaii is the 43rd largest state.

Population

1,455,271
(2020)

STATE FLAG

Hawaii's flag is red, white, and blue. In the upper left corner is the British flag. Originally King Kamehameha I had used the Union Jack alone as the flag of Hawaii. This was to show the friendship between his kingdom and Britain. Years later, the eight horizontal stripes were added. They stand for Hawaii's eight main islands.

INDUSTRY

Main Exports

aircraft parts   shrimp   macadamia nuts

bottled water   fruit juice

JOBS

MANUFACTURING
2%

FARMING AND NATURAL RESOURCES
2%

GOVERNMENT
20%

SERVICES
76%

Natural Resources
fertile soil, rocks and sand, water

GOVERNMENT

Federal Government
2 REPRESENTATIVES | **2** SENATORS

HI

4 ELECTORAL VOTES

USA

State Government
51 REPRESENTATIVES | **25** SENATORS

STATE SYMBOLS

STATE BIRD
NENE

STATE ANIMAL
MONK SEAL

STATE FLOWER
YELLOW HIBISCUS

STATE TREE
KUKUI (CANDLENUT TREE)

archipelago—a group of islands

canyon—a deep and narrow valley that has steep sides

colonists—people sent by a government to a new region or territory

coral reefs—structures made of coral that usually grow in shallow seawater

culture—the beliefs, arts, and ways of life in a place or society

heritage—the traditions, achievements, and beliefs that are part of the history of a group of people

hurricanes—storms formed in the tropics that have violent winds and often have rain and lightning

lava tube—a cave formed from cooled lava; lava is melted rock from a volcano.

lei—a necklace or wreath usually made of flowers

missionaries—people sent to a place to spread a religious faith

plantations—large farms that grow coffee beans, cotton, rubber, or other crops; plantations are mainly found in warm climates.

Polynesia—islands of the central and southern Pacific Ocean; Hawaii is part of Polynesia.

rain forest—a thick, green forest that receives a lot of rain

snorkel—to swim near the surface while breathing through a long tube called a snorkel

taro—a tropical Asian plant grown for its edible starchy stem which is often ground into flour or cooked as a vegetable

tourism—the business of people traveling to visit other places

traditional—related to customs, ideas, or beliefs handed down from one generation to the next

tropical—related to the tropics; the tropics is a hot, rainy region near the equator.

volcanoes—holes in the earth; when a volcano erupts, hot ash, gas, or melted rock called lava shoots out.

AT THE LIBRARY

Calkhoven, Laurie. *Duke Kahanamoku*. New York, N.Y.: Simon Spotlight, 2017.

Hamalainen, Karina. *Hawai′i Volcanoes*. New York, N.Y.: Children's Press, 2019.

Lyon, Drew. *Surfing, Wakeboarding and Other Extreme Water Sports*. North Mankato, Minn.: Capstone Press, 2020.

ON THE WEB

FACTSURFER

Factsurfer.com gives you a safe, fun way to find more information.

1. Go to www.factsurfer.com.

2. Enter "Hawaii" into the search box and click 🔍.

3. Select your book cover to see a list of related content.